My Family

Guided/Group Reading Notes

Pink Band

Contents

Introduction 2

Guided/Group reading notes

① Character story: *Tiger's Family*
by Shoo Rayner 12

② Character story: *Go to Bed!*
by Alex Lane 18

③ Character non-fiction: *Ducks*
by Alex Lane 24

④ Variety story: *Is Dad in Here?*
by Alex Lane 30

⑤ Variety non-fiction: *My Family*
by Emma Lynch 36

OXFORD

Introduction

Learning in the Foundation Stage – an integrated approach

Young children do not learn in neatly divided curriculum areas. The six areas of learning identified in the *Statutory Framework for the Early Years Foundation Stage* (SFEYFS) are frequently integrated within the experiences and activities undertaken by young children. Many of the activities or experiences undertaken in early years' settings help to develop skills and understanding across several areas. This reflects how learning develops in the home – through the experiences and activities of everyday life. Young children learn by doing, rather than being told. Learning is a shared process and children's learning is enhanced by the support of a knowledgeable and trusted adult (within the home and the early years' setting). Learning is also enhanced when the child is actively involved and interested. In effective early years' settings there is a balance of freely chosen or child-initiated activities and adult-led activities, with opportunities for indoor and outdoor play.

Project X and learning in Reception/Primary 1

The thematic approach of the Project X books supports an integrated approach to learning. The themed clusters of books in each band provide possibilities to enhance personal, social and emotional development; problem solving, reasoning and numeracy; creative development; physical development and knowledge and understanding of the world, along with a major focus on developing communication, language and literacy. In guided/group reading sessions, you will want to encourage children to make links beyond the book they are reading to other books in the cluster and other texts and experiences concerning families.

The Project X character stories allow readers to make links between characters, events and actions across the books. This enables young children to build a growing understanding of characters, to give reasons why things happen and see how characters may change and develop. It can help them recognize cause and effect. Longer term, it helps children reflect on the skill of determining importance, as a minor incident or detail in one book may prove to have greater significance when considered across several books.

These *Guided/Group Reading Notes* offer specific suggestions for each book within the **My Family** cluster which embed communication, language and literacy learning within an active and interactive approach. The following example activities would help provide a rich, integrated learning context within which the guided/group reading of any/all of the books can be located. As part of ongoing child- and adult-initiated play and learning:
- Share stories, songs, rhymes and poems about families. Include the use of props or puppets to encourage retelling.
- Encourage children to make up their own poems about families and use storytelling in play.
- Engage children in role-play.
- Provide small world figures, animals and buildings for children to create 'family' environments such as farms and wildlife parks.
- Provide quiet places to share a collection of books and pictures about families, including animal families.
- Listen and watch audiovisual materials on families. The Project X *Interactive Stories* software contains materials you could use for this. *Go to Bed* from the **My Family** cluster is included on the CD-ROM for Reception/Y1.

Further suggestions for the integration of the six areas of learning within each themed cluster of books are contained in the *Teaching Handbook* for Reception/P1.

Texts at **pink band** contain natural language, which closely follows children's speech patterns. The key word is 'familiarity' – not only in terms of language, but in terms of settings, objects and events. The text and illustrations are highly motivating and enable the child to become involved through repetition, rhyme, exploring sounds and patterned language. There are opportunities for children to identify common words and to read simple phonetically regular words. These words should give children the opportunity to apply their newly developing letter-sound correspondence. Simple sentences are used and illustrations provide full support for the text. The cluster contains stories with a clear beginning, middle and ending to help support children's growing knowledge of story structure. The non-fiction books contain some simple non-fiction features such as headings, labels and the use of photographs.

Progression in the Project X character books

In this cluster, readers are introduced to two of the series characters – Max and Tiger – and build up knowledge of their families and lives. Some of the distinctive characteristics of the friends are beginning to develop – such as Tiger's love of food and Max's relationship with his sister.

In *Tiger's Family* we meet Tiger and the rest of his family, including his pet cat. In *Go To Bed!* we meet Max and his younger sister, Molly. Both books show some of the characteristic behaviours of the children and their relationships with other members of their family.

At pink band, readers are introduced to the series characters, but these characters do not yet shrink. The shrinking adventures begin at red band.

Communication, language and literacy CLL

The development and use of communication and language are central to young children's learning. From our earliest days, sounds and body language, and later speech, enable us to communicate our needs and feelings. Oral language underpins the development of thinking. It allows us to share, interrogate, comment and reflect on our experiences. As we develop reading and writing skills, these provide further means to enhance our learning and communication. Early years' settings should provide a rich communication, language and literacy environment to support the development of speaking, listening, reading and writing. Early reading experiences (including guided/group reading) are embedded in and supported by such an environment. The *Teaching Handbook* for Reception/P1 gives further detail on the elements of a rich communication, language and literacy curriculum.

Speaking, listening and drama

These *Guided/Group Reading Notes* contain suggestions for speaking, listening, group interaction and role play for each book in the *My Family* cluster. These activities develop children's skills in these areas and offer them opportunities to articulate their thinking and feelings and thus enhance their understanding of the texts.

Learning about how books work

As children are beginning to learn to read, they will not necessarily understand the conventions of reading yet. They will still be learning about concepts of print, such as what a letter is and what a word is. Guided reading at this stage should provide children with opportunities to learn and practise skills such as left to right directionality, book handling, simple prediction, understanding meaning, matching print to spoken word and locating familiar words.

Decoding texts

Project X recognizes that knowledge of the alphabetic code and the skill of blending are important skills in developing early reading. The books offer opportunities to practise and apply skills taught in phonics programmes through reading interesting and lively texts. In order to support progression in knowledge of the alphabetic code and the skill of blending, some of the vocabulary in bands pink to yellow is carefully aligned to the sequence of phonemes likely to be taught in a systematic phonics programme. A chart showing this alignment is provided in the *Teaching Handbook* for Reception/P1. Details of the decodable vocabulary and other vocabulary in the **My Family** cluster are given in the vocabulary chart on pages 10 and 11. Other vocabulary in the books includes context words supported by the pictures or meaning, names and natural language patterns.

Building vocabulary

Explicit work on enriching vocabulary and encouraging an interest in words and their meanings is important in building children's communication skills and their understanding of what they read. Repeatedly encountering a word and its variants helps it become known. The thematic 'cluster' structure of Project X supports this because words are repeated within and across the books. Suggestions for vocabulary work are included in these *Guided/Group Reading Notes*.

Building comprehension

Understanding what we have read is at the heart of reading and is central to children's motivation. Comprehension should be encouraged from children's earliest encounters with print. The crucial concept that print carries meaning is what gives purpose to the act of reading. Enjoyment and seeing a purpose to reading helps children, especially boys, remain motivated and eager to

learn. These *Guided/Group Reading Notes* contain practical strategies to develop the following important aspects of comprehension:
- Previewing
- Predicting
- Activating and building prior knowledge
- Questioning
- Recall
- Visualizing and other sensory interpretations
- Deducing, inferring and drawing conclusions
- Determining importance
- Synthesizing
- Empathizing
- Summarizing
- Personal response, including adopting a critical stance.

Not every aspect of comprehension is covered in each cluster. The research basis and rationale for focusing on these aspects of comprehension is given in the *Teaching Handbook* for Reception/P1.

The guided/group reading sessions

The engaging content and careful levelling of Project X books makes them ideal for use in guided/group reading sessions.

Guided/group reading sessions offer opportunities for children to practise their developing reading skills in a supportive context. They offer teachers a context in which to support children as they apply and practise reading strategies and teach both the group and individuals at the point of need. They provide opportunities to observe, listen and assess. Discussion before and after reading helps children understand what they have read and articulate personal responses.

To use the books in guided/group reading sessions, you should select a level that creates a small degree of challenge for the group of pupils. The *Teaching Handbook* for Reception/P1 contains a chart showing the approximate reading level for each colour band.

Typically children should be able to read about 90% of the book unaided. This level of 'readability' provides the context for children to practise their reading and build reading confidence. The 'challenge' in the text provides opportunities for explicitly teaching reading skills.

These *Guided/Group Reading Notes* give many ideas for follow-up activities. Some of these can be completed within the guided/group reading session. Some are longer activities that will need to be worked on over time. It is not expected that you would complete all the suggested activities. Guided/group reading sessions should be relatively brief in Reception/P1 and you may wish to undertake some of the suggested further activities at another point.

Talking, visualising and reading as a way into writing

The Project X books provide both models and inspiration to support mark making and writing. The oral activities and role play suggested in these *Guided/Group Reading Notes* also often have the potential for extension into writing activity. Suggestions for relevant, contextualized and interesting mark making or writing activities are given in the follow-up activities.

Home/school reading

Parents are vital partners in developing children's reading enjoyment, confidence and enthusiasm. Books used in a guided/group reading session can also be used in home/school reading programmes. Following a guided/group reading session, the child could reread the book at home to build reading confidence and fluency. Advice for parents in supporting their child in reading is provided on the inside covers of individual books. Further advice for teachers concerning home/school reading partnerships is given in the *Teaching Handbook* for Reception/P1.

Assessment

During guided/group reading, teachers observe, listen and make ongoing assessments of individuals and of the group. Early learning goals and literacy objectives are indicated for each book and you should assess against these. Select just one or two at a time as a focus for your assessments. The same early learning goals and literacy objectives can be assessed over several reading sessions. You may also wish to track back to earlier statements in the *Early Years Foundation Stage Profile* (*EYFSP*).

Continuous reading objectives and ongoing assessment

The following objectives will be supported in every guided reading session and are therefore a *continuous* focus for attention and assessment:

- Hear and say sounds in words in the order in which they occur SFEYFS p.13, PNS 5.4
- Read simple words by sounding out and blending the phonemes all through the word from left to right. PNS 5.5
- Read a range of familiar and common words and simple sentences independently. PNS 5.9, SFEYFS p.13

Further objectives are given with the notes for each book. Early learning goals from other areas of learning are also included.

Correlation to the specific objectives within the Scottish, Welsh and Northern Ireland curricula are provided in the *Teaching Handbook* for Reception/P1.

The assessment chart for the **My Family** cluster is provided in the *Teaching Handbook* for Reception.

Vocabulary chart

The pink band books offer opportunities for children to practise and apply their decoding skills, develop comprehension and build their enjoyment of reading. The vocabulary for practising and applying decoding skills is indicated below. Readers widen their vocabulary through encountering new words in the context of a story or information text. These are also indicated. Some of context words are decodable but are likely to be beyond children's current phonic knowledge. 'Tricky' words are high and medium frequency words that contain phonemes not yet likely to have been taught.

Tiger's Family	Decodable words (phonemes in sets 1–7)	is, sad, has, bad, mad, Mum
	Phonic focus: rhyming CVC words	Dad, mad, sad, bad
	Tricky words	no
	Context words	Moggy, Tiger, Toby, cakes, more, glad
Go To Bed!	Decodable words (phonemes in sets 1–7)	got, up, bed
	Phonic focus: VC and CVC words	up, got, bed
	Tricky words	go, to
	Context words	Molly, Max, went, goodnight

Ducks	Decodable words (phonemes in sets 1–7)	a, mum, dad, sits, on, has, duck(s), him, can, eggs
	Phonic focus: 2 letters making 1 sound	duck, eggs
	Tricky words	the, look, are
	Context words	makes, nest, born, grow, baby, hatch, later, swim
Is Dad in Here?	Decodable words (phonemes in sets 1–7)	is, Dad, in, not, yes
	Phonic focus: VC, CV and CVC words	in, is, Dad, not, yes
	Tricky words	no, here
My Family	Decodable words (phonemes in sets 1–7)	Kim, can, run, hop, Ben, Mum, Dad, run, Nan, nap, Tom
	Phonic focus: CVC words	can, run, Kim, hop, Ben, Mum, Dad, run, Nan, Tom, nap
	Tricky words	I, me
	Context words	family, spin, jump, my

Tiger's Family

BY SHOO RAYNER

About this book

This book introduces Tiger's family, including his pet cat.

You will need

- *Families* Photocopy Master, *Teaching Handbook* for Reception/P1
- Children's family photographs

Literacy goals and objectives
 	
Early learning goals (Communication, language and literacy) from Statutory Framework for the Early Years Foundation Stage (SFEYFS) Literacy Framework objectives (PNS)
	○ Listen with enjoyment, and respond to stories, songs and other music, rhymes and poems and …
	  • make up their own stories, songs, rhymes and poems (SFEYFS, p.13, PNS 2.1)
	  • sustain attentive listening and respond with relevant comments, questions or actions (SFEYFS, p.13, PNS 8.1)
	○ Show an understanding of the elements of stories, such as main character, sequence of events, and openings (SFEYFS p.13, PNS 7.3)
	○ Read some high frequency words (PNS 5.7)

Linking letters and sounds (decoding and phonics Phonic focus: rhyming CVC words	○ Hear and say sounds in words in the order in which they occur (SFEYFS p.13, PNS 5.4) ○ Read simple words by sounding out and blending the phonemes all through the word from left to right (PNS 5.5)
Related early learning goals ○ Creative development ○ Personal, social and emotional development	○ Use their imagination in art and design, music, dance, imaginative and role play and stories (SFEYFS p.16) ○ Maintain attention, concentrate, and sit quietly when appropriate (SFEYFS p.12)

NB. Before this guided/group reading session, ask the children to bring in photographs of their own family members. Display them, ensuring that each relationship to the child is labelled clearly for others to read.

Before reading

To activate prior knowledge and encourage prediction

- Talk with the children about their families. Who do they live with? Discuss extended families and what they like to do together. Look at the front cover and discuss who each of these people might be. Which person do you think Tiger is? How might the other people be related to Tiger? (**activating prior knowledge, predicting**)
- Tell the children that the story is about Tiger and his family.

To engage readers, introduce new vocabulary and support fluent reading

- Give children the cut-out pictures from the *Families* Photocopy Masters and allow them to play a game of 'Happy families' to explore vocabulary related to families.

To support decoding and word recognition

- Depending on the phonic work you have been undertaking, select one or two of the words from the book (see vocabulary chart on page 10) and remind the children how to sound and blend phonemes.

During reading

- Depending on your usual practice and the group you are working with, you may wish to:
  - Read the book to the children. As you read, ask children to follow with their fingers, pointing to each word as it is read. Check that the children are keeping up and pointing to the right word. Model using expression to emphasize the significance of the rhyme and rhythm.
  - Take it in turns to read a page. Model reading a page and then ask the children to read a page.
  - Invite them to read the whole book independently.
- If you have not already done so, remind the children what to do if they encounter a difficult word. Model with an example from the book if necessary, sounding out and blending the letter sounds. Praise children who successfully decode unfamiliar words.

> **Assessment point**
>
> Can the children
> - Read a range of familiar and common words and simple sentences independently?
> - Sound out and blend phonemes all through the word from left to right when they encounter new words?

After reading

Returning to the text
- You may wish to quickly reread the story to the children to enhance their engagement and understanding.
- Ask if they enjoyed the story. What was their favourite part? (**personal response**)
- Talk with the children about the main events in the story. Can they recall the sequence of events? (**recall, summarizing**)
- Who are the main characters in the story and how are they related? (**recall**)
- Why did Dad get angry with Tiger? (**empathizing**)

> **Assessment point**
>
> Can the children explain the main events of the story in a clear sequence?

Building comprehension
- Set up a home corner in the role play area. Invite the children to explore consequences of actions through play. What would have happened in their home if they had knocked the cakes on to the floor? Would their mum just make some more? (**empathizing, deducing, inferring and drawing conclusions**)
- Talk about Tiger and Toby's relationship. Do the children think the boys get on? Are they well behaved? (**deducing, inferring and drawing conclusions**)

Building fluency
- Depending on the group you are working with, you might wish to ask the children to reread the story to a friend or family member.

Follow-up activities

Literacy activities

- **ⓐ Phonic opportunity** Skim through the book and ask children to collect examples of rhyming words, e.g. *glad*, *mad*, *sad*, *bad*. What other words can they think of that rhyme with these words? Ask the children to sound the words and identify each phoneme in the words. Can they identify which phonemes make the words rhyme? Work together to write a list and focus on the phonemes used to make the initial and final sounds.

- Develop children's speaking and listening through role play by exploring the relationships in Tiger's family. (**CLL**)

Tiger is bad.

Later ...
Mum has more cakes.

Other activities

- Ask the children to talk with their families about their different relations. They could bring in their own family trees and display them in class. (**KUW**)

- During circle time, discuss what constitutes good behaviour and consequences of actions. What happens if the children do not follow rules? Why do we have rules? (**PSED**)

- Bake cakes in class. Allow the children to explore the different ingredients and to investigate what happens when things are heated. Discuss different types of measures, e.g. grams, etc. (**KUW, PSRN**)

Go To Bed!

BY ALEX LANE

About this book
This book tells the story of Max and his sister Molly who is unable to go to sleep until she has checked for monsters.

You will need
- *Making words* Photocopy Master, *Teaching Handbook* for Reception/P1

Literacy goals and objectives Early learning goals (Communication, language and literacy) from the Statutory Framework for the Early Years Foundation Stage (SFEYFS) Literacy Framework objectives (PNS)	○ Listen with enjoyment, and respond to stories, songs and other music, rhymes and poems and … • make up their own stories, songs, rhymes and poems (SFEYFS, p.13, PNS 2.1) • sustain attentive listening and respond with relevant comments, questions or actions (SFEYFS, p.13, PNS 8.1) ○ Show an understanding of the elements of stories, such as main character, sequence of events, and openings (SFEYFS p.13, PNS 7.3) ○ Read some high frequency words (PNS 5.7)
Linking letters and sounds (decoding and phonics) **Phonic focus:** VC and CVC words	○ Read simple words by sounding out and blending the phonemes all through the word from left to right (PNS 5.5)
Related early learning goals ○ Creative development ○ Personal, social and emotional development ○ Knowledge and understanding of the world	○ Respond in a variety of ways to what they see, hear, smell, touch and feel (SFEYFS p.16) ○ Maintain attention, concentrate and sit quietly when appropriate (SFEYFS p.12) ○ Find out about, and identify, some features of living things, objects and events they observe (SFEYFS p.14)

Before reading

To activate prior knowledge

- Talk with the children about bedtime. What is their bedtime? What do they do at bedtime? Do they read a story? Who reads stories to them? Do they like bedtime? What do they not like about bedtime? How do they feel about going to bed? Is there anything that makes them scared at bedtime? **(activating prior knowledge)**
- Ask the children to point to the title of the book.
- Tell the children that this story is about Max and his sister Molly at bedtime.

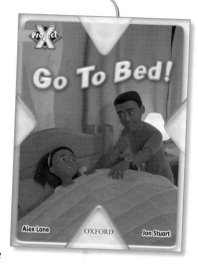

To engage readers and support fluent reading

- Model reading the story to the children by reading pages 3–5. Demonstrate how to use your voice to give expression when reading the speech bubbles.
- What do the children think might happen next? **(predicting)**

> **Assessment point**
>
> Can the children make sensible predictions about what might happen in a text?

To support decoding and word recognition

- Depending on the phonic work you have been undertaking, select one or two of the words from the book (see vocabulary chart on page 10) and remind the children how to sound and blend phonemes.

> **Assessment point**
>
> Can the children orally blend and segment CVC words?

During reading

- Depending on your usual practice and the group you are working with, you may wish to:
  - Read the book to the children. As you read, ask children to follow with their fingers, pointing to each word as it is read. Check that the children are keeping up and pointing to the right word. Model using expression to emphasize the significance of the rhyme and rhythm.
  - Take it in turns to read a page. Model reading a page and then ask the children to read a page.
  - Invite them to read the whole book independently.
- If you have not already done so, remind the children what to do if they encounter a difficult word. Model with an example from the book if necessary, sounding out and blending the letter sounds. Praise children who successfully decode unfamiliar words.

> **Assessment point**
>
> Can the children
> - Read a range of familiar and common words and simple sentences independently?
> - Sound out and blend phonemes all through the word from left to right when they encounter new words?

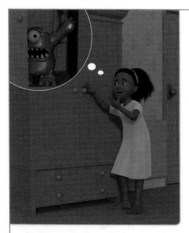

Molly got up.

Go to bed Molly!

After reading

Returning to the text
- You may wish to quickly reread the story to the children to enhance their engagement and understanding.
- Ask if they enjoyed the story. What was their favourite part? (**personal response**)
- Ask the children:
  - Why did Molly not want to go to sleep? (**recall**)
  - What did Molly need to do before she could go to sleep? (**recall, deducing, inferring and drawing conclusions**)
  - Why could Max not sleep? (**deducing, inferring and drawing conclusions**)

> **Assessment point**
>
> Can the children show understanding of the main character in the story, i.e. why Max could not go to sleep?

- Make a bedroom in the role play or home corner. Encourage children to play together to explore bedtime. What happens if they cannot get to sleep? What frightens them at night? (**empathizing**)
- Ask the children to draw a picture of something that might frighten them when they are trying to go to sleep. Talk about how members of the family make them feel better. (**visualizing, empathizing**)

Follow-up activities

Literacy activities

- Read bedtime stories, such as 'The Baby Who Wouldn't Go to Bed' *by Helen Cooper* and 'Milo and the Night Market' *by Angela McAllister*, and share the children's favourite bedtime stories. (**CLL**)
- Sing lullabies that help the children to sleep. (**CLL**)
- Make up oral stories using puppets to help Molly to sleep. (**CLL**)
- Watch the story on the *Interactive Stories* CD-ROM. (**CLL**)
- Use the phoneme frame and letters on the *Making words* Photocopy Master to blend and segment some of the VC and CVC words from the story. You could also make other CVC words. (**CLL**)

Max and Molly went to bed.

Other activities

- Talk about dreams and nightmares. What dreams have the children had? Children might like to draw a picture storyboard of their dreams. Discuss nightmares and what the children do to make themselves feel better. (**PSED**)

- Talk about night and day. Where does the moon go? Create shadows on the wall, letting the children's imagination run. What are the different shadows? How are the shadows created? Discuss how one's imagination can create all sorts of different images. (**KUW**)

- Talk about the time that the children go to bed. How long did it take for both children in the story to go to bed? Talk about digital and analogue clocks. (**PSRN**)

Ducks

BY ALEX LANE

About this book
This non-fiction book explores the life cycle of ducks – how they are born and raised.

You will need
- *How many eggs?* Photocopy Master, *Teaching Handbook* for Reception/P1
- Small world animals with their babies

Literacy goals and objectives Early learning goals (Communication, language and literacy) from Statutory Framework for the Early Years Foundation Stage (SFEYFS) Literacy Framework objectives (PNS)	○ Use language to imagine and recreate roles and experiences (PNS 8.3) ○ Show an understanding of how information can be found in non-fiction texts to answer questions about where, who, why and how (PNS 7.3) ○ Read some high frequency words (PNS 5.7)
Linking letters and sounds (decoding and phonics) **Phonic focus:** two letters making one sound	○ Read simple words by sounding out and blending the phonemes all through the word from left to right (PNS 5.5)
Related early learning goals ○ Creative development ○ Knowledge and understanding of the world ○ Problem solving, reasoning and numeracy	○ Use their imagination in art and design, music, dance, imaginative and role play and stories (SFEYFS p.16) ○ Find out about, and identify, some features of living things, objects and events they observe (SFEYFS p.14) ○ Count reliably up to ten everyday objects. (SFEYFS p.14) ○ Talk about and recognize simple patterns (SFEYFS p.14)

NB. If you have the opportunity to visit a pond and observe ducks prior to reading this book it would help children's knowledge and understanding.

Before reading

To activate prior knowledge and encourage prediction

- Look at the front cover. Ask the children to point to the title. Can they use their phonic knowledge to decode the title? What type of bird is in the picture? What do children already know about ducks? **(activating prior knowledge)**

- Can they think of other things they would like to find out about ducks?

> **Assessment point**
>
> Can the children generate questions that they would like to find out about from this non-fiction text?

To support decoding and word recognition

- Depending on the phonic work you have been undertaking, select one or two of the words from the book (see vocabulary chart on page 11) and remind the children how to sound and blend phonemes.

During reading

- Depending on your usual practice and the group you are working with, you may wish to:
  - Read the book to the children. As you read, ask children to follow with their fingers, pointing to each word as it is read. Check that the children are keeping up and pointing to the right word. Model using expression to emphasize the significance of the rhyme and rhythm.
  - Take it in turns to read a page. Model reading a page and then ask the children to read a page.
  - Invite them to read the whole book independently.
- If you have not already done so, remind the children what to do if they encounter a difficult word. Model with an example from the book if necessary, sounding out and blending the letter sounds. Praise children who successfully decode unfamiliar words.

> **Assessment point**
>
> Can the children
> - Read a range of familiar and common words and simple sentences independently?
> - Sound out and blend phonemes all through the word from left to right when they encounter new words?

The baby ducks are born.   The baby ducks grow.

The duck sits on the eggs.

Later ...

Look!

The eggs hatch.

After reading

Returning to the text

- Ask the children:
  - Did you like this book? What part did you like the most? (**personal response**)
  - What new facts have you found out about ducks? (**recall, summarizing**)
  - How do you think the ducks might make a nest? (**deducing, inferring and drawing conclusions**)
  - Do you know what type of book this is? How is it different from a story book?
  - Why do you think that someone has written a book about ducks? (**deducing, inferring and drawing conclusions**)
  - Why do we need information books? (**determining importance**)

> **Assessment point**
>
> Can the children talk about the differences between fiction and information books? Do they realize that information is more likely to be found in a non-fiction text rather than a story book?

27

Follow-up activities

Literacy activities

- Talk about different vocabulary used for the names of different adult and baby animals. (**CLL**)
- Learn songs about animals and their babies. (**CLL**)
- Learn counting songs, e.g. 'Five little ducks went swimming one day'. (**CLL**)
- Make a collaborative fact sheet about ducks. (**CLL**)
- Explore relationships between animals using puppets and small world resources. (**CLL**)
- ⓓ **Phonic opportunity**. Tell children that some words have two letters that make one sound, e.g. *duck*, *egg*. Help children to segment and blend the words. Ask the children to write the words in the air to help them visualize the words. Encourage children to make up sentences with the words in them and read them to the group. Remind them to write the words as accurately as they can.

The duck sits on the nest.   The duck has eggs.

The duck has 7 eggs!

Other activities

- Provide small world resources to explore animal life cycles and adult/baby relationships, e.g. caterpillars and butterflies, tadpoles and frogs, cats and kittens, hens and chicks, cows and calves, etc. (**KUW**)
- What materials would be good to make a nest? Provide different materials such as leaves, tissue, sticks, plastic, etc. Can children weave the materials together to make a nest? Which nest is most comfortable and why? Which materials make the best nest? (**KUW**, **CD**)
- Ask the children to count the eggs in the nests on the *How many eggs?* Photocopy Master. Then help them to cut out the eggs at the bottom of the sheet and play games in pairs, such as snap. They could then try sorting and classifying the eggs according to size and pattern. (**PSRN**)

Is Dad in Here?

BY ALEX LANE

About this book
This book tells the story of a puppy who has lost his dad.

You will need
- *Animals and their babies* Photocopy Master, *Teaching Handbook* for Reception/P1
- *Is Dad in here?* Photocopy Master, *Teaching Handbook* for Reception/P1
- Puppy or dog puppet
- Small world resources: puppy, horse, frog, lady, dog (and other farmyard animals/people), farm play mat

Literacy goals and objectives	
Early learning goals (Communication, language and literacy) from Statutory Framework for the Early Years Foundation Stage (SFEYFS) Literacy Framework objectives (PNS)	o Listen with enjoyment, and respond to stories, songs and other music, rhymes and poems and ... • make up their own stories, songs, rhymes and poems (SFEYFS, p.13, PNS 2.1) • sustain attentive listening and respond with relevant comments, questions or actions (SFEYFS, p.13, PNS 8.1) o Show an understanding of the elements of stories, such as main character, sequence of events, and openings (SFEYFS p.13, PNS 7.3) o Retell narratives in the correct sequence, drawing on the language patterns of stories (SFEYFS p.13, PNS 7.4) o Read some high frequency words (PNS 5.7)
Linking letters and sounds (decoding and phonics) Phonic focus: CV, VC and CVC words	o Read simple words by sounding out and blending the phonemes all through the word from left to right (PNS 5.5)
Related early learning goals o Creative development o Personal, social and emotional development	o Use their imagination in art and design, music, dance, imaginative and role play and stories (SFEYFS p.16) o Maintain attention, concentrate and sit quietly when appropriate (SFEYFS p.12)

Before reading

To activate prior knowledge, engage readers and introduce new vocabulary

- Look at the picture on the front cover. Do the children think this is an adult dog or a puppy? (**deducing, inferring and drawing conclusions**)
- Draw children's attention to the question mark. Explain that this title is a question. Ask the children to work in pairs to think about what the puppy might be asking. (**predicting**) You could introduce a puppet of a dog or puppy at this point and let the children ask him/her questions.

To support decoding and word recognition

- 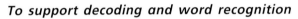**Phonic opportunity** Practise blending CVC words with the children, such as *Dad*, *not* and *yes*.
- Alternatively, depending on the phonic work you have been undertaking, select one or two of the words from the book (see vocabulary chart on page 11) and remind the children how to sound out and blend phonemes.
- You may also wish to point out some of the high or medium frequency words or practise decoding some of the phonically regular words in this book and listed in the vocabulary chart on page 11.

During reading

- Depending on your usual practice and the group you are working with, you may wish to:
  - Read the book to the children. As you read, ask children to follow with their fingers, pointing to each word as it is read. Check that the children are keeping up and pointing to the right word. Model using expression to emphasize the significance of the rhyme and rhythm.
  - Take it in turns to read a page. Model reading a page and then ask the children to read a page.
  - Invite them to read the whole book independently.
- If you have not already done so, remind the children what to do if they encounter a difficult word. Model with an example from the book if necessary, sounding out and blending the letter sounds. Praise children who successfully decode unfamiliar words.

> **Assessment point**
>
> Can the children
> - Read a range of familiar and common words and simple sentences independently?
> - Sound out and blend phonemes all through the word from left to right when they encounter new words?

No. Dad is not in here.   Is Dad in here?

After reading

Returning to the text
- Ask the children if they liked the story. What was their favourite part? (**personal response**)
- Ask the children to find the different questions that are asked in the book. What do they notice about the questions? (They all have a question mark.)
- Look at page 4 together. What happens when the puppy runs into the kitchen? How do the children think the lady is feeling? Now look at page 6. Talk about what happened in this picture. How do the animals feel? How does the puppy feel? Do the same for the horse on page 8. (**empathizing**)
- What do they think the lady, frog and horse might want to say to the little puppy? What questions might they ask the puppy? (You could use the dog/puppy puppet and let children explore the things the characters might want to say.) (**empathizing, questioning**)
- Encourage the children to begin to draw conclusions about the puppy's character. (**deducing, inferring and drawing conclusions**)

> **Assessment point**
>
> Can the children display an awareness of the feelings and needs of others?

- If you have small world characters, encourage children to explore what might happen when the little puppy meets them. What other chaos could he cause on the farm? (**visualizing**)
- Show children the map of the farm on the *Is Dad in Here?* Photocopy Master. Can they work out where the puppy went to look for his dad? Where else could he have looked? (**visualizing, predicting**)

Follow-up activities

Literacy activities

- **ⓐ Phonic opportunity** Encourage the children to recognise key words: *dad*, *is*, *no* and *in*. For fun you may like to play a game whereby the children make a barking sound each time they spot a key word! **(CLL)**
- Draw pictures of the puppy looking in a different place. Encourage the children to write a simple sentence about where the dog is looking. **(CLL)**
- Use puppets to explore dialogue between the puppy and other animals when he is lost. What different questions might he ask? **(CLL)**

No. Dad is not in here.   Is Dad in here?

Other activities

- If you have a farm play mat or similar, use small world materials and ask children to imagine what might happen when the puppy looks in other places, e.g. pig sty, chicken run, etc.
- Play hide and seek. How do children feel when they can't find someone? Have they ever lost their mum or dad? How did it make them feel? (**PSED**)
- Ask the children to choose one of the different places where the puppy looks for his dad and use available art materials to make a picture. You could then make a class book or display the pictures to show an extended story. (**CD**)
- Cut out the picture cards on the *Animals and their babies* Photocopy Master. Show children the cards and play a game by showing the children a card and asking the children to put their hands up to name the matching adult or baby animal. The child who answers correctly can keep the card. (**KUW**)

My Family

BY EMMA LYNCH

About this book
This book introduces a family and describes the different things they can do.

You will need
- *We can ...* Photocopy Master, *Teaching Handbook* for Reception/P1
- Sports equipment
- Children's family photographs

Literacy goals and objectives Early learning goals (Communication, language and literacy) from the Statutory Framework for the Early Years Foundation Stage, (SFEYFS) Literacy Framework objectives (PNS)	○ Use talk to organize, sequence and clarify thinking, ideas, feelings and events (SFEYFS, p.13, PNS 1.2) ○ Show an understanding of how information can be found in non-fiction texts to answer questions about where, who, why and how (PNS 7.3) ○ Read some high frequency words (PNS 5.7)
Linking letters and sounds (decoding and phonics) **Phonic focus:** CVC words	○ Read simple words by sounding out and blending the phonemes all through the word from left to right (PNS 5.5)
Related early learning goals ○ Physical development ○ Problem solving, reasoning and numeracy	○ Move with control and coordination (SFEYFS p.15) ○ Say and use number names in order in familiar contexts (SFEYFS p.14)

NB. Before this guided/group reading session, ask the children to bring in photographs of their own family members. Display them, ensuring that each relationship to the child is labelled clearly for others to read.

Before reading

To activate prior knowledge and encourage prediction

- Ask the children to show the group the photographs of their family. Work with the children to make miniature displays of their family – on a pin board, in a booklet or on a poster, etc. Talk about the different family members, how they are related and what they are like. What do they like to do? (**activating prior knowledge**)
- Look at the front cover and explain to the children that these are all pictures of members of one family. Can the children work out the relationships between each? Encourage them to use appropriate vocabulary to label the pictures, e.g. son, daughter, brother, sister, etc. (**predicting**)

To support decoding and word recognition

- **ⓓ Phonic opportunity** Practise blending CVC words with the children, such as *can*, *run*, *hop*, *jog*, *nap*.
- **ⓓ Phonic opportunity** Alternatively, depending on the phonic work you have been undertaking, select one or two of the words from the book (see vocabulary chart on page 11) and remind the children how to sound out and blend phonemes.

During reading

- Depending on your usual practice and the group you are working with, you may wish to:
  - Read the book to the children. As you read, ask children to follow with their fingers, pointing to each word as it is read. Check that the children are keeping up and pointing to the right word. Model using expression to emphasize the significance of the rhyme and rhythm.
  - Take it in turns to read a page. Model reading a page and then ask the children to read a page.
  - Invite them to read the whole book independently.
- If you have not already done so, remind the children what to do if they encounter a difficult word. Model with an example from the book if necessary, sounding out and blending the letter sounds. Praise children who successfully decode unfamiliar words.

> **Assessment point**
>
> Can the children
> - Read a range of familiar and common words and simple sentences independently?
> - Sound out and blend phonemes all through the word from left to right when they encounter new words?

After reading

Returning to the text

- You may wish to quickly reread the book to the children to enhance their engagement and understanding.
- Discuss any comments and questions the children might have. (**personal response, questioning**)
- Ask some 'who' and 'what' questions, e.g. Who likes to hop? What can Ben do? (**recall**)
- Discuss whether this is a factual book or a story book. How do the children know? (**deducing, inferring and drawing conclusions**)

> **Assessment point**
>
> Do the children understand how information to answer 'who' and 'what' questions can be found in non-fiction texts?

Kim can hop.

Ben can jump.

Follow-up activities

Literacy activities
- Ask the children to use the *We can ...* Photocopy Master to write simple sentences about what their family or class members like to do. You could model the writing on this pattern: 'Nana can sleep. This is Nana sleeping.' (**CLL**)
- Talk with the group about what they like doing. What are their favourite activities? Do they have interests in common with other class members?

Other activities
- Encourage the children to try some of the different activities, e.g. hopping, jumping, running and spinning. (**PD**)
- Carry out different tests of how children can do things, e.g. for how long can they run on the spot? How high can they jump? (**PSRN, PD**)
- Make a class bar graph of who can hop, jump, skip. etc. (**PSRN**)
- Can the children use their family pictures to make their own family tree, similar to the one on pages 10–11?